LOW-CARB COMFORT FOOD

60+ Low-Carb Comfort Food Recipes

SARAH HARDY

MY MONTANA KITCHEN

TABLE OF CONTENTS

My name is Sarah, and you can find me at mymontanakitchen.com where I help women remove barriers to their success, build healthy habits and feed their families delicious, fail-proof recipes every day of the week!

I believe you can still enjoy delicious food - even if you're trying to cut carbs!

This book is filled with over 50 lower-carb, delicious, comfort-food recipes that your entire family will love.

Download your FREE BONUS ebook!

Substitutions & Ingredients

BAKING BLEND

In each recipe that calls for Baking Blend, I'm referencing the Trim Healthy Mama Baking Blend. This is the blend used to calculate the nutritional information. You can order the THM Blend on Amazon or trimhealthymama.com.

MAKE YOUR OWN BAKING BLEND

You can make a DIY baking blend by making up your own mix of equal parts Almond Flour, Coconut Flour, and Flax Meal. (The nutritional information will vary a bit from the printed nutritional information when using the homemade blend.)

Taco Chicken Casserole

Nutrition - 1/6th of recipe
Calories: 476 | Carbohydrates: 6g | Protein: 50g | Fat: 23g | Fiber: 3g

SERVINGS: 6

INGREDIENTS

- 5 Cups Diced Cooked Chicken Breast
- 1 12 Ounce Bag Frozen Riced Cauliflower
- ½ Cup Chopped Onion
- 1/4 Cup Chopped Jalapeno
- 1 ½ Cups Sour Cream
- 1 Cup Salsa
- 4 Tablespoons Taco Seasoning
- 1 Cup Shredded Cheddar Cheese

INSTRUCTIONS

1. Preheat oven to 350.
2. In a large bowl, combine chicken, cauliflower, onion, jalapeno, sour cream, salsa, and taco seasoning.
3. Stir well, then spread into a 9x13 dish.
4. Top with shredded cheddar cheese.
5. Bake for 30-35 minutes, broiling the last minute or two to brown the cheese on top a bit.

King Ranch Chicken Casserole

Nutrition - 1/10th of recipe

Calories: 341 | Carbohydrates: 9g | Protein: 28g | Fat: 21g |
Fiber: 2g

SERVINGS: 10

INGREDIENTS

- 5 Cups Cooked Boneless Skinless Chicken Breast , cubed
- 1 Tablespoon Olive Oil
- 1 Package (8 Ounce) Mushrooms , sliced
- 1 Small Onion , diced
- 1 Red Bell Pepper , seeded and diced
- 1 Green Bell Pepper , seeded and diced
- 4 Ounces Cream Cheese , room temperature
- 1 Cup Chicken Broth
- 1 Can (10 Ounce) Diced Tomatoes With Green Chilies
- 2 Tablespoons Taco Seasoning
- 2 Cups Shredded Colby-Jack Cheese , divided

- 1 Cup Sour Cream
- 1/2 Cup Heavy Cream
- 1/2 Teaspoon Xanthan Gum
- Salt And Pepper to taste
- 2 Tablespoons Cilantro , chopped

INSTRUCTIONS

1. Preheat oven to 350.
2. In a large bowl, combine chicken, cauliflower, onion, jalapeno, sour cream, salsa, and taco seasoning.
3. Stir well, then spread into a 9x13 dish.
4. Top with shredded cheddar cheese.
5. Bake for 30-35 minutes, broiling the last minute or two to brown the cheese on top a bit.

Parmesan Chicken Casserole

Nutrition - 1/10th of recipe
Calories: 288 | Carbohydrates: 5g | Protein: 32g | Fat: 15g | Fiber: 1g

SERVINGS: 10

INGREDIENTS

- 5 Cups Cooked Chicken cubed or shredded
- 1 24 Ounce Marinara Sauce I like the Rao's brand
- 1 1/2 Cups Grated Parmesan Cheese divided
- 1 1/2 Cups Shredded Mozzarella Cheese
- 1/2 Cup Almond Flour

INSTRUCTIONS

1. Preheat the oven to 350 degrees.
2. Spray a 9x13 casserole dish with nonstick cooking spray.
3. In a large bowl, combine cooked chicken, half of the marinara sauce, 1 cup of parmesan, and 1 cup of mozzarella cheese (see notes below for an alternative).
4. Spread the mixture in the casserole dish.
5. Pour the remaining marinara over the top of the casserole.
6. Sprinkle the remaining mozzarella and parmesan over the marinara and then top with the almond flour.
7. Cover with foil and bake for 30 minutes or until the cheese is melted and bubbling.

Notes
You can substitute 2 cups of shredded Italian blend cheese for the grated parmesan and shredded mozzarella.

Greek Chicken Casserole

Nutrition - 1/12th of recipe
Calories: 233 | Carbohydrates: 3g | Protein: 9g | Fat: 20g |
Fiber: 0g

SERVINGS: 12

INGREDIENTS

- 3 Cups Boneless Skinless Chicken Breast cut into bite-size pieces
- 1 Can Artichoke Hearts, drained
- 1 Cup Roasted Red Peppers, drained
- 1 Cup Kalamata Olives, halved
- 1 Zucchini, ends removed, halved, and sliced in 1-inch pieces
- 1 Cup Mozzarella Cheese, shredded

For the dressing:

- 1/2 Cup Olive Oil
- 1/4 Cup Red Wine Vinegar
- 1/4 Teaspoon Salt
- 1 Teaspoon Garlic Powder
- 1 Teaspoon Dried Oregano Leaves

INSTRUCTIONS

1. Preheat the oven to 350 degrees. Prepare a 9x13 casserole dish with nonstick cooking spray.
2. In a small bowl or jar, mix together the ingredients for the dressing.
3. Place the chicken in a gallon zip-top freezer bag. Add half of the dressing and mix with the chicken. Let the chicken rest on the counter for 20 minutes or in the refrigerator up to overnight.
4. Transfer the chicken to the casserole dish.
5. Over the chicken, place the vegetables and olives. Pour the remaining dressing over the top. Toss the vegetables with the chicken to coat evenly.
6. Top the casserole with the mozzarella cheese.
7. Bake for 45 minutes or until the chicken is done.

Alfredo Chicken Casserole

Nutrition - 1/6th of recipe
Calories: 466 | Carbohydrates: 6g | Protein: 33g |
Fat: 32g | Fiber: 3g

SERVINGS: 6

INGREDIENTS

- 8 Ounces Cream Cheese Softened
- 1/2 Cup Heavy Whipping Cream
- 1/2 Cup + 2 Tablespoons Parmesan, Divided I use the green can kind
- 1/2 Teaspoon Basil
- 1/2 Teaspoon Salt
- 2.5 Cups Cooked Chicken cubed or shredded
- 2 Tablespoons Minced Garlic
- 1/2 Cup Chopped Onion
- 16 Ounce Bag Frozen Cauliflower
- 10 Ounce Bag Frozen Spinach
- 1 Cup + 1/2 Cup Shredded Mozzarella cheese, Divided

INSTRUCTIONS

1. Preheat oven to 350.
2. In a large bowl, beat softened cream cheese, heavy whipping cream, 1/2 cup Parmesan, basil, and salt until mixed well.
3. Add chicken, minced garlic, chopped onion, frozen cauliflower, frozen spinach, and 1 cup shredded Mozzarella cheese.
4. Mix until well combined.
5. Pour mixture into a greased 9x13 dish and top with remaining 1/2 cup Mozzarella cheese and 2 tablespoons Parmesan cheese.
6. Bake for 35-45 minutes, or until casserole is bubbly and cheese begins to brown on top.

Chicken Fajita Casserole

Nutrition - 1/12th of recipe
Calories: 228 | Carbohydrates: 4g | Protein: 23g |
Fat: 14g | Fiber: 1g

SERVINGS: 12

INGREDIENTS

- 2 lbs. Chicken Breasts, cooked and shredded (about 3.5 - 4 cups)
- 1 Tablespoon Coconut Oil, optional
- 2 Bell peppers, eeded and sliced
- 1 Large or 2 Small Onion, sliced
- 1 (8 ounce) Package Cream Cheese, softened
- 1 Tablespoon Taco Seasoning
- 2 Cups Shredded Monterey Jack Cheese

INSTRUCTIONS

1. Preheat oven to 350 degrees.
2. Prepare a 9x13 casserole dish with coconut oil cooking spray.
3. In a large skillet over medium-high heat, add coconut oil and swirl to coat.
4. Add onions and peppers to skillet, cooking over medium-high heat and stirring occasionally until softened. Remove from heat.
5. To the skillet, add shredded chicken, cream cheese, taco seasoning, and 1 cup cheese. Stir to combine.
6. Transfer to casserole dish.
7. Top casserole with remaining cheese.
8. Bake for 25 to 30 minutes or until cheese is melted and bubbling.

Jalapeno Popper Chicken Casserole

Nutrition - 1/9th of recipe
Calories: 370 | Carbohydrates: 4g | Protein: 24g |
Fat: 30g | Fiber: 1g

SERVINGS: 9

INGREDIENTS

- 3 Cups Shredded Cooked Chicken Breast
- ½ Cup (or more, if desired) Chopped Jalapeños
- 8 oz. Cream Cheese, Softened
- 1/2 Cup Mayonnaise
- 2 Teaspoons Garlic Powder
- 2 Teaspoons Onion Powder
- 1 Cup Shredded Cheddar Cheese
- Additional ½ Cup Sliced Jalapeños
- ½ Cup Real Bacon Pieces

INSTRUCTIONS

1. Preheat oven to 350.
2. In a large mixing bowl, combine all ingredients except shredded cheese, bacon and additional sliced jalapeños.
3. Pour mixture into a 9x13 pan and top with 1 cup shredded cheese and bacon pieces.
4. Bake for 30-35 minutes, or until cheese just starts to brown. (I broiled mine for a couple minutes at the end.)

Green Chile Chicken Casserole

Nutrition - 1/6th of recipe
Calories: 417 | Carbohydrates: 6g | Protein: 32g |
Fat: 30g | Fiber: 1g

SERVINGS: 6

INGREDIENTS

- 8 Ounces Cream Cheese, Softened
- ¾ Cup Sour Cream
- 1 7 Ounce Can Diced Green Chiles
- ½ Teaspoon Cumin
- ¼ Teaspoon Salt
- 3 Cups Diced or Shredded Chicken
- 1 ¼ Cups Shredded Cheese of choice, Divided

INSTRUCTIONS

1. Preheat oven to 350.
2. In a large bowl, mix all ingredients together, reserving ¼ cup shredded cheese.
3. Spread mixture into an 8x8 glass dish.
4. Sprinkle reserved ¼ cup of cheese over top of casserole.
5. Bake for 35-40 minutes, or until cheese is golden, and casserole is bubbly.

Buffalo Chicken Casserole

Nutrition - 1/6th of recipe
Calories: 613 | Carbohydrates: 8g | Protein: 33g |
Fat: 47g | Fiber: 1g

SERVINGS: 6

INGREDIENTS

- 3 Cups Cooked Chicken Diced or Shredded
- ½ Cup Mayonnaise
- 1 8 Ounce Package Cream Cheese Softened
- ½ Cup + 1 Tablespoon Hot Sauce
- 1 12 Ounce Bag Frozen Cauliflower Florets
- 1 Cup Loose Frozen Spinach
- 1 Cup Shredded Cheddar Cheese
- ½ Teaspoon Salt
- ½ Teaspoon Italian Seasoning
- 1 ½ Teaspoons Garlic Powder
- 1 Teaspoon Onion Powder

For the Topping:
- ½ Cup Shredded Mozzarella Cheese
- ¼ Cup Crumbled Blue Cheese

INSTRUCTIONS

1. Preheat oven to 350.
2. In a large mixing bowl, mix together all the ingredients for the casserole.
3. Spread into a 9x13 baking dish.
4. Top with Shredded Mozzarella Cheese and Crumbled Blue Cheese.
5. Bake for 35-40 minutes, or until casserole is bubbly and cauliflower is cooked through - see note below. (I like to broil mine for the last several minutes.)

Notes
If you use the frozen cauliflower florets, you will need to bake it for at least 40 minutes - perhaps a touch longer. If using the cauliflower rice, you shouldn't need to bake it quite as long.

Spaghetti Squash Chicken Tetrazzini

Nutrition - 1/6th of recipe

Calories: 262 | Carbohydrates: 10g | Protein: 26g |

Fat: 14g | Fiber: 3g

SERVINGS: 6

INGREDIENTS

- 2 Cups Cooked Spaghetti Squash
- 2 Cups Cooked Chicken Breast
- 1 Tablespoon Butter
- 1/2 Cup Chopped Onion
- 3 Garlic Cloves Minced
- 2 Cups Fresh Sliced Mushrooms
- 3 Tablespoons Baking Blend*
- 1 Cup Chicken Broth
- 1 Cup Half & Half
- 3/4 Teaspoon Thyme
- 1 Teaspoon Basil
- 1/2 Teaspoon Salt
- 1/4 Teaspoon Black Pepper
- 1/2 Cup Grated Parmesan Cheese the green can
- 1/2 Cup Shredded Cheese Any kind you prefer

*See note on Substitutions page about Baking Blend

INSTRUCTIONS

1. Preheat oven to 350.
2. In a medium skillet, melt butter.
3. Add chopped onion and minced garlic and sautee for 2-3 minutes.
4. Add sliced mushrooms. Cook and stir until mushrooms begin to soften.
5. Sprinkle Baking Blend over onion/mushroom mixture and stir to coat.
6. Add chicken broth, half and half, thyme, basil, salt and pepper.
7. Bring to a boil, then reduce heat and simmer for 3-4 minutes, or until sauce begins to thicken.
8. Add parmesan cheese and stir well. Remove from heat.
9. Place spaghetti squash and cooked chicken into a greased, 2 quart dish. (Mix well)
10. Pour cream sauce over spaghetti squash/chicken mixture.
11. Top with 1/2 Cup shredded cheese.
12. Bake for 25 - 30 minutes, or until bubbly. (I broiled mine for a couple minutes at the end,)

Cheesy Chicken & Broccoli Casserole

Nutrition - 1/6th of recipe
Calories: 530 | Carbohydrates: 9g | Protein: 32g |
Fat: 41g | Fiber: 2g

SERVINGS: 6

INGREDIENTS

- 3 Cups Shredded Cooked Chicken Breast
- 5 Cups Chopped Fresh Broccoli
- 8 oz. Cream Cheese Softened
- 1 Cup Sour Cream
- 1/2 Cup Mayonnaise
- 1 Teaspoon Garlic Salt
- 1 Teaspoon Onion Powder
- 1/2 Teaspoon Basil
- 1/4 Teaspoon Smoked Paprika
- 1/4 Teaspoon Rosemary
- 1/4 Teaspoon Thyme
- 1 Cup Shredded Cheese I used Mozzarella, but you can use any kind

INSTRUCTIONS

1. Preheat oven to 350.
2. In a large mixing bowl, combine all ingredients except shredded cheese.
3. Pour mixture into a 9x13 pan and top with 1 cup shredded cheese.
4. Bake for 30-35 minutes, or until cheese just starts to brown. (I broiled mine for a couple minutes at the end.)

Cheesy Chicken Vegetable Casserole

Nutrition - 1/9th of recipe
Calories: 342 | Carbohydrates: 9g | Protein: 27g |
Fat: 22g | Fiber: 2g

SERVINGS: 9

INGREDIENTS

- 1 8 Ounce Cream Cheese, Softened
- 1 Cup Cottage Cheese, pureed in a blender - see note below
- 1/2 Cup Sour Cream
- 1/2 Cup Grated Parmesan Cheese, the green can kind is fine
- 1 1/2 Cups Shredded Cheddar Cheese
- 2 Cups Frozen Spinach
- 1 Medium Zucchini, Diced
- 1 Small/Medium Yellow Squash, Diced
- 1/4 Small Onion, Diced (Optional)
- 1 Teaspoon Onion Powder
- 1 Teaspoon Garlic Powder
- 1 Teaspoon Mineral Salt
- 3 Cups Cooked Chicken Breast, Diced or Shredded

INSTRUCTIONS

1. Preheat oven to 350.
2. In a large bowl, mix all the ingredients except 1/2 Cup shredded Cheddar cheese.
3. Pour into a 9x13 pan and top with the remaining cheese.
4. Bake for 25-30 minutes, or until casserole is hot and bubbly.

Notes

I chose to use pureed cottage cheese to ease the caloric load just a bit. Using the cottage cheese also adds an extra bump of protein. If the idea of using cottage cheese turns you off, feel free to use mayo or sour cream (or a mixture of both) in its place.

I measure the spinach when it is frozen, and I do not thaw it before mixing it.

Chicken Spaghetti

Nutrition - 1/12th of recipe
Calories: 209 | Carbohydrates: 14g | Protein: 12g |
Fat: 10g | Fiber: 4g

SERVINGS: 12

INGREDIENTS

- 3 to 4 cups (about 1 ½) Cooked Spaghetti Squash
- 3 Cups Cooked and Shredded Chicken
- 2 (10 ounce) Cans Diced Tomatoes with Green Chilies
- 1 (8 ounce) Package Cream Cheese, Softened
- 1 Cup Sour Cream
- 1 Cup Shredded Sharp Cheddar Cheese, Divided
- ½ Teaspoon Garlic Powder
- 1 Teaspoon Salt
- ½ Teaspoon Pepper

INSTRUCTIONS

1. Cook spaghetti squash: Preheat oven to 400 degrees. Carefully cut the spaghetti squash in half and remove seeds and membranes from the core.

2. Brush inside spaghetti squash with refined coconut oil and season with salt and pepper.

3. Place the cut side down on a baking sheet prepared with aluminum foil. Pierce a small hole through the back of the spaghetti squash.

4. Cook for 45 minutes, or until the squash is tender (but not mushy).

5. Scoop squash from the peel and pull into strands using two forks.

6. Reduce oven heat to 350 degrees. Prepare a 9x13 casserole dish with nonstick coconut cooking spray.

7. In a large bowl, mix chicken, diced tomatoes and green chilies, cream cheese, sour cream, ½ cup cheddar cheese, garlic powder, salt, and pepper.

8. Carefully fold in spaghetti squash to avoid mushing the strands.

9. Transfer to a casserole dish and cover with remaining cheese.

10. Bake for 30 minutes or until the cheese begins to turn golden on the edges and the casserole is hot and bubbling.

Easy Cashew Chicken

Nutrition - 1/8th of recipe
Calories: 288 | Carbohydrates: 8g | Protein: 27g |
Fat: 17g | Fiber: 2g

SERVINGS: 8

INGREDIENTS

- 2 Pounds Boneless Skinless Chicken Thighs
- Salt And Pepper To Taste
- 1 Tablespoon Olive Oil
- 1 Green Bell Pepper Seeded And Cut Into 1-Inch Pieces
- 1 Red Bell Pepper Seeded And Cut Into 1-Inch Pieces
- 1 Onion Seeded And Cut Into 1-Inch Pieces
- 2 Cups Frozen Broccoli
- 2 Teaspoons Rice Wine Vinegar
- 3 Tablespoons Liquid Aminos
- 1 1/2 Teaspoons Sesame Oil
- 1 Teaspoon Ground Ginger
- 2 Cloves Garlic, Minced
- 2 Teaspoons Chili Sauce (look for a no-sugar variety)
- 1/2 Cup Cashews
- Sliced Green Onions For Garnish

INSTRUCTIONS

1. Preheat the oven to 350 degrees. Prepare a 9x13 casserole dish with nonstick cooking spray.
2. In a large skillet over medium-high heat, add the olive oil. Season the chicken with salt and pepper. Add the chicken to the skillet in batches and brown on all sides.
3. Transfer chicken to the casserole dish.
4. In the casserole dish, toss the chicken together with the bell peppers, broccoli, and onions.
5. In a mason jar or small bowl, mix together the rice wine vinegar, liquid aminos, sesame oil, ground ginger, and chili garlic sauce.
6. Pour the mixture over the chicken and vegetables, then sprinkle with cashews.
7. Cover and cook for 30 minutes. Remove the cover and continue cooking for 15 minutes.
8. Garnish with sliced green onions. Serve over cauliflower rice, if desired.

Creamy Ham & Broccoli Casserole

Nutrition - 1/6th of recipe
Calories: 441 | Carbohydrates: 11g | Protein: 19g |
Fat: 36g | Fiber: 3g

SERVINGS: 6

INGREDIENTS

- 2 Cups Diced Ham
- 2 14 Ounce Bags Frozen Broccoli
- 8 oz. Cream Cheese Softened
- 1 Cup Plain Greek Yogurt
- 1/2 Cup Mayonnaise
- 1 Teaspoon Garlic Salt
- 1 Teaspoon Onion Powder
- 1/2 Teaspoon Basil
- 1/2 Teaspoon Smoked Paprika
- 1/4 Teaspoon Rosemary
- 1/4 Teaspoon Thyme
- 1 Cup Shredded Cheese (any kind is fine)

INSTRUCTIONS

1. Preheat oven to 350.
2. In a large bowl, combine all ingredients except shredded cheese and pork rinds.
3. Pour mixture into a greased 9x13 glass pan.
4. Top with shredded cheese.
5. Bake, uncovered for 45-60 minutes, or until casserole is bubbling and cheese is beginning to brown on top.

Notes

You may notice pork rinds in the photo. But to be honest, I don't know if I would use them again. They really didn't add much as far as crunch or flavor to the casserole, and I think it would be just as tasty without them! If you want to use them, feel free to add them to the top of the casserole before baking, but they are not an essential part of the recipe!

Cabbage Roll Casserole

Nutrition - 1/8th of recipe
Calories: 316 | Carbohydrates: 15g | Protein: 29g |
Fat: 17g | Fiber: 4g

SERVINGS: 8

INGREDIENTS

- 2 Pounds Ground Beef
- 1 Onion , diced
- 3 Cloves Garlic , minced
- 2 Cans (15 ounce) Tomato Sauce
- 1 Teaspoon Dried Thyme Leaves
- 1/2 Teaspoon Dried Dill
- 1/4 Teaspoon Ground Sage
- 1/2 Teaspoon Salt
- 1/2 Teaspoon Black Pepper
- 1/4 Teaspoon Ground Cayenne
- 1 Head Cabbage , cored and coarsely chopped
- 1 Cup Mozzarella Cheese

INSTRUCTIONS

1. Preheat the oven to 375 degrees. Prepare a 9x13 casserole dish with nonstick cooking spray.
2. In a large skillet over medium-high heat, cook the ground beef with the onion, crumbling the beef as it cooks. When the beef is no longer pink, stir in the garlic. Drain the beef well and return to the skillet.
3. Add 1 can of tomato sauce to the skillet with the dry seasonings. Stir and simmer over medium-high heat for 2 to 3 minutes.
4. In a large mixing bowl, combine the ground beef sauce and cabbage, stirring until the cabbage is coated in the sauce.
5. Transfer the combination to the prepared baking dish. Top with the remaining can of tomato sauce.
6. Cover the dish with aluminum foil and bake for 45 minutes.
7. Remove te aluminum foil and add the cheese in an even layer.
8. Return the casserole to the oven and continue baking for 10 minutes or until the cheese has melted.

Philly Cheesesteak Casserole

Nutrition - 1/12th of recipe

Calories: 333 | Carbohydrates: 3g | Protein: 28g | Fat: 23g | Fiber: 0g

SERVINGS: 12

INGREDIENTS

- 2 Pounds Ground Beef, browned and drained
- 1 Tablespoon Coconut Oil, optional
- 2 Bell Peppers, seeded and sliced
- 1 Large or 2 Small Onions, sliced
- 1 (8 ounce) Package Cream Cheese, softened
- ½ Teaspoon Garlic Powder
- Salt and Pepper, to taste
- 12 Slices Provolone Cheese

INSTRUCTIONS

1. Preheat oven to 350 degrees.
2. Prepare a 9x13 casserole dish with coconut oil spray.
3. In a large skillet, brown ground beef over medium-high heat and chop into crumbles.
4. Drain ground beef to remove grease.
5. If grease is removed from skillet, add coconut oil and swirl to coat the pan.
6. Add onions and peppers to skillet, cooking over medium-high heat and stirring occasionally until softened. Remove from heat.
7. To the skillet, add cooked ground beef, cream cheese, garlic powder, salt and pepper. Stir to combine. Transfer to casserole dish.
8. Top casserole with slices of provolone cheese.
9. Bake for 25 to 30 minutes or until cheese is melty and bubbling.

Cheesy Cabbage Casserole

Nutrition - 1/6th of recipe
Calories: 306 | Carbohydrates: 7g | Protein: 22g |
Fat: 21g | Fiber: 3g

SERVINGS: 6

INGREDIENTS

- 1 ½ Pounds Ground Beef
- ½ Medium Cabbage, Shredded
- 2 Tbsp Butter, Unsalted
- 5 Strips of Bacon
- 1 Teaspoon Basil
- ½ Teaspoon Thyme
- 1 Teaspoon Oregano
- ½ Teaspoon Rosemary
- 2 Cups Shredded Cheddar Cheese
- Salt and pepper to taste
- Freshly Chopped Parsley, Optional

INSTRUCTIONS

1. Preheat the oven to 425 degrees.
2. Cook the bacon until crispy in a skillet over medium-high heat. Remove the bacon from the skillet, crumble it, and reserve 1 tbsp of the bacon grease in the skillet.
3. Add 2 tbsp of butter to the bacon grease in the skillet, and add the crumbled bacon back in.
4. Place the shredded cabbage in the skillet, and stir to coat it in the butter and bacon grease.
5. Pour the cabbage mixture into the bottom of a greased casserole dish.
6. In the same skillet, add the ground beef, and cook until completely browned over medium-high heat.
7. Mix in the oregano, thyme, rosemary and basil, as well as salt and pepper to taste.
8. Layer the cooked beef over the top of the cabbage in the casserole dish.
9. Top the mixture with 2 cups of shredded cheddar cheese.
10. Bake the casserole for 15-20 minutes until the cheese is browned and bubbly on top.
11. Sprinkle with freshly chopped parsley and serve.

Pizza Meatball Casserole

SERVINGS: 8 servings

Nutrition - 4 Meatballs

Calories 328 | Total Fat 19g | Total Carbohydrates 8g | Dietary Fiber 3g | Protein 32g

For the Meatballs:

- 1.5 Pounds Lean Ground Beef
- ¼ Cup Finely Chopped Onion
- 3 Tablespoons Nutritional Yeast
- 2 Eggs
- ¼ Teaspoon Thyme
- 1 Teaspoon Garlic Powder
- 1 Tablespoon Parsley
- ¼ Cup Golden Flaxmeal
- 3 Tablespoons Heavy Cream or Unsweetened Almond Milk
- 1 Teaspoon Salt
- ¼ Teaspoon Black Pepper

For the Pizza Sauce: (Or you can use your favorite pre-made pizza sauce - you need 2 cups)

- 1 6 ounce can Tomato Paste
- 1 Teaspoon Garlic Powder
- ½ Teaspoon Garlic Salt
- 2 Teaspoons Oregano
- 1 Teaspoon Basil
- 1 Teaspoon Olive Oil
- 1 "doonk" Pure Stevia 1/32 of a teaspoon
- 1 ¼ Cup Water

For the Toppings:

- 32 Pieces Pepperoni
- 1 Cup Shredded Mozzarella Cheese

1. Preheat oven to 350.
2. Make Meatballs
3. In a large bowl, mix all meatball ingredients well.
4. Using a cookie scoop (or your hands) form meat mixture into golf ball sized balls and place in a 9x13 casserole dish.
5. Place one piece of pepperoni on each meatball.
6. Make Pizza Sauce
7. Mix all pizza sauce ingredients together.
8. Pour sauce over meatballs.
9. Top with cheese.
10. Bake for 30-40 minutes, or until cheese is melty and meatballs are cooked through.

Cheeseburger Pie

Nutrition - 1/9th of recipe
Calories: 333 | Carbohydrates: 3g | Protein: 21g |
Fat: 25g | Fiber: 0g

SERVINGS: 9

INGREDIENTS

- 1 ½ Pound Ground Beef
- 1 Small Onion, chopped
- ½ Teaspoon Garlic Powder
- ½ Teaspoon Dry Mustard
- ½ Teaspoon Black Pepper
- ½ Teaspoon Salt
- 6 eggs
- 1 Cup Heavy Cream
- 1 Cup Shredded Cheddar Cheese

INSTRUCTIONS

1. Preheat oven to 350 degrees. Spray a 9 inch round or 8x8 inch square casserole dish with coconut oil cooking spray.
2. Cook the ground beef/chuck with the onion. Drain well.
3. Spread the beef mixture evenly in the baking dish.
4. In a mixing bowl, whisk together the seasonings, eggs, and heavy cream. Slowly pour over the beef mixture so it sinks into the meat.
5. Top casserole with cheese.
6. Bake for 30 to 35 minutes or until the center is set. Allow the casserole to rest about 5 minutes before slicing.
7. Serve with cheeseburger toppings like pickles, mustard, lettuce, tomato, bacon, etc.

Loaded Cauliflower Casserole with Bacon

Nutrition - 1/6th of recipe

Calories: 390 | Carbohydrates: 13g | Protein: 17g | Fat: 32g | Fiber: 3g

SERVINGS: 6

INGREDIENTS

- 2 (12 ounce) Bags Frozen Cauliflower and Broccoli Mix
- 2 to 4 Slices Bacon
- 1 Onion, Diced
- ⅔ Cups Sour Cream
- 8 Ounces Cream Cheese, Softened
- ½ Teaspoon Garlic Powder
- ½ Teaspoon Black Pepper
- 2 Cups Shredded Sharp Cheddar Cheese, divided
- Green Onion, Sliced as Garnish

INSTRUCTIONS

1. Preheat oven to 350.
2. Spray a 2 quart baking dish with coconut oil cooking spray.
3. In a large skillet, cook bacon until cooked through, then remove bacon to paper towels to drain.
4. Add onion to bacon grease and cook over medium heat until onions are translucent and fragrant. Drain onions on paper towels.
5. Cook cauliflower/broccoli mix according to package directions and drain well.
6. In a large mixing bowl, mix together softened cream cheese, sour cream, 1 cup cheddar cheese, garlic powder, and black pepper.
7. Mix cream cheese mixture with cooked vegetables. Spread in baking dish. Top with remaining cheddar cheese.
8. Bake for 25 to 30 minutes.
9. Chop cooked bacon and sprinkle over top with sliced green onion.

Cheesy Yellow Squash Casserole

Nutrition - 1/6th of recipe
Calories: 272 | Carbohydrates: 12g | Protein: 17g |
Fat: 21g | Fiber: 9g

SERVINGS: 6

INGREDIENTS

- 2 Medium Crookneck Yellow Squash, Sliced (about 3-4 cups)
- 1 Cup Shredded Mozzarella Cheese
- 1 Cup Shredded Cheddar Cheese
- 1 ½ Teaspoons Italian Seasoning

For the Topping:

- 1 Recipe Low Carb Biscuits
- 1/2 Teaspoon Oregano
- 1/2 Teaspoon Onion Powder
- 1/2 Teaspoon Garlic Powder

INSTRUCTIONS

1. Preheat oven to 350.
2. Mix up Low Carb Biscuit dough, adding the oregano, onion powder, and garlic powder to the dough.
3. In a 2 quart baking dish, place a layer of squash in the bottom.
4. Top with 1/3 of the cheese, and 1/3 of the Italian seasonings.
5. Repeat layers two more times.
6. Drop biscuit dough on top of squash mixture.
7. Bake for 40 - 45 minutes, or until biscuits are golden brown. (You want to bake it at least 40 minutes to ensure that the biscuits are cooked through.)

Cheesy "Potato" Casserole

Nutrition - 1/6th of recipe
Calories: 277 | Carbohydrates: 8g | Protein: 10g |
Fat: 23g | Fiber: 2g

SERVINGS: 6

INGREDIENTS

- 5 Cups Peeled and Diced Daikon Radish
- Water for boiling the radish + salt
- ¼ Cup Diced Onion
- 1 Tablespoon your favorite chicken bullion powder
- 4 Ounces Cream Cheese Softened
- 1 Cup Sour Cream
- 2 Cups Shredded Cheese - Sharp Cheddar is great

INSTRUCTIONS

1. Preheat oven to 375.
2. Place peeled and dished radishes in a medium pot, and fill with enough salted water to cover the radishes.
3. Boil for 25 - 30 minutes, or until radishes are easily pierced with a fork.
4. Drain well, and rinse with cold water.
5. Place drained radishes in a bowl, add remaining ingredients and mix well.
6. Place into an 8x8 baking dish and bake for 30 minutes.
7. Broil for another 1-3 minutes, watching carefully so as not to burn the top.

Notes
It is very important that you peel the radish completely. The peeling has a "woody" texture.

Cauliflower Bacon Chowder

Nutrition - 1/4th of recipe
Calories: 209 | Carbohydrates: 14g | Protein: 12g |
Fat: 10g | Fiber: 4g

SERVINGS: 4

INGREDIENTS

- 6 Slices Bacon, cut into pieces
- 1 Onion, diced
- 1/2 Cup Carrots, sliced
- 1/2 Cup Celery, diced
- 2 Cloves Garlic, minced
- 1/2 Teaspoon Dried Oregano Leaves
- 1/2 Teaspoon White Pepper
- 1/2 Teaspoon Salt
- 1 Head Cauliflower, stem removed and coarsely chopped
- 2 to 3 Cups Vegetable or Chicken Broth, depending on the consistency desired
- 1/4 Cup Cream Cheese

INSTRUCTIONS

1. In a medium stock pot, cook bacon over medium heat until crisp. Remove bacon and drain on paper towels.
2. Add the onion, carrots, and celery to the pot. Cook for 3 to 5 minutes or until softened, scraping any browned pieces from the bottom of the pot with a wooden spoon. Stir in the garlic, oregano, pepper, and salt.
3. Add the cauliflower and 2 cups of broth to the pot. Heat to boiling and cook for approximately 15 minutes or until cauliflower is tender.
4. Add cream cheese to the soup and stir until melted and combined.
5. Using an immersion blender, puree about half of the soup. Check the consistency and add additional broth if desired. Heat through.
6. Serve topped with cooked bacon and/or cheese.

Pizza Soup

Nutrition - 1/8th of recipe
Calories: 361 | Carbohydrates: 11g | Protein: 26g | Fat: 23g | Fiber: 4g

SERVINGS: 8

INGREDIENTS

- 1 16 ounce Package Italian sausage, casings removed
- 1 Pound Lean Ground Beef
- 1 8 ounce Package Baby Bella Mushrooms, diced
- 2 Cloves Garlic, minced
- 1 Zucchini cut through the length and then in 1 inch slices
- 1/2 Red Bell Pepper seeded and diced
- 1 Tablespoon Italian seasoning
- 1 32 Ounce container Beef Broth
- 1 15 Ounce can Diced Tomatoes in juice
- 1 6 Ounce can Tomato Paste
- 3 Cups Kale, coarsely chopped
- 4 Ounces Cream Cheese room temperature, softened
- 1/4 Cup Heavy Cream

INSTRUCTIONS

1. Brown the meats in a skillet or in the electric pressure cooker using the saute function. Drain well.
2. In the electric pressure cooker, add the meats, mushrooms, garlic, zucchini, red bell pepper, seasoning, and beef broth. Stir together until blended.
3. Add the diced tomatoes and tomato paste. Do not stir.
4. Place the lid on the electric pressure cooker and set the valve to sealing. Cook on the "pressure cook" or "manual" setting for 15 minutes. Turn the valve for a quick release.
5. Into the soup, stir the cream cheese until melted. Add the kale and heavy cream. Stir to blend and allow the kale to wilt.
6. Serve topped with mozzarella cheese, grated parmesan, sliced pepperoni, and/or sliced black olives.

Jambalaya

Nutrition - 1/6th of recipe
Calories: 497 | Carbohydrates: 16g | Protein: 34g |
Fat: 16g | Fiber: 7g

SERVINGS: 6

INGREDIENTS

- 2 Tablespoons Olive Oil
- 1 Pound Andouille or Kielbasa Sausage thinly sliced
- 2 Bell Peppers diced
- 1/2 Large Onion diced
- 1/2 Cup Celery diced
- 3 Garlic Cloves minced
- 1 Pound Shrimp peeled, deveined and thawed
- 4 Cups Riced Cauliflower (frozen or fresh work)
- 1 14 oz. Can Diced Tomatoes
- 1/4 Cup Chicken Broth
- 2 Tablespoons Cajun Seasoning
- 1 Teaspoon Sea Salt
- Green Onions and fresh Parsley diced for garnish

INSTRUCTIONS

1. Heat the oil in a large pot or dutch oven over medium heat. Add the bell peppers, onions, and celery. Saute for 5-7 minutes, or until the vegetables are soft.

2. Add the sausage and saute for another 4-5 minutes, until the sausage is lightly browned.

3. Add the minced garlic. Cook for 1 minute.

4. Add the remaining ingredients (except for shrimp and cauliflower rice) and mix well.

5. Bring close to a boil, then lower the heat and simmer uncovered for 10 minutes.

6. Add the cauliflower and shrimp and cook until shrimp is cooked through, and liquid is reduced, about 5-7 more minutes.

7. Remove from heat and serve hot with sliced green onions and parsley.

Chicken Taco Soup

Nutrition - 1/5th of recipe
Calories: 407 | Carbohydrates: 8g | Protein: 22g |
Fat: 31g | Fiber: 2g

SERVINGS: 5

INGREDIENTS

- 1 Pound Chicken Thighs
- 1 Small Onion, Diced
- 2 Cloves Garlic, Minced
- 1 (10 ounce) can Diced Tomatoes with Chilies
- 1 Tablespoons Tomato Paste
- 1 Tablespoon Ground Cumin
- 1 teaspoon Chili Powder
- ½ teaspoon Salt
- 2 cups Chicken Broth
- 1 (8 ounce) package Cream Cheese
- ½ cup Cheddar Cheese, plus more for garnish
- Chopped Cilantro for garnish

INSTRUCTIONS

1. Place everything in the liner of an electric pressure cooker EXCEPT cream cheese, cheddar cheese, and cilantro.

2. Cover and seal the electric pressure cooker. Cook on manual or "pressure cook" for 18 minutes. Quickly release the pressure and carefully remove the lid.

3. Using two forks, shred the chicken. If you prefer the chicken to not be shredded, remove the chicken and dice before returning to the soup.

4. Turn the electric pressure cooker to saute. Stir in the cream cheese and cheddar until the cheeses are melted.

5. Serve with additional cheddar and chopped cilantro.

Notes
You can also make this on the stovetop - follow the same basic instructions, but simply simmer on the stove.

Broccoli Cheddar Soup

Nutrition - 1/6th of recipe
Calories: 364 | Carbohydrates: 8g | Protein: 15g |
Fat: 29g | Fiber: 2g

SERVINGS: 6

INGREDIENTS

- 4 Tablespoons Butter
- ½ Cup Diced White Onion
- 1 Clove Garlic, Minced
- 3 ½ Cups Chicken Broth
- 4 Cups Broccoli, Coarsely Chopped
- Salt and Pepper, to Taste
- ½ Cup Heavy Cream
- 2 Cups Shredded Cheddar Cheese
- ½ Teaspoon Xanthan Gum

INSTRUCTIONS

1. In a medium stockpot, melt butter over medium-high heat. Add the onion and garlic and cook until softened, about 3 minutes.
2. Add the chicken broth and broccoli. Bring to a boil and reduce heat to medium. Allow broccoli to simmer until softened.
3. Add salt and pepper as desired.
4. Add the heavy cream and return the soup to a boil. Then, remove the pot from heat and stir in the cheddar cheese, scraping the bottom of the pot. (The cheese may cling to the broccoli.)
5. Sprinkle xanthan gum over the soup and stir to combine. Allow the soup to rest knowing that it will continue to thicken as it cools.
6. Serve alone or topped with crumbled bacon, additional cheddar, freshly ground black pepper, and/or sliced green onions.

Pressure Cooker Chili

Nutrition - 1 Cup
Calories: 271 | Carbohydrates: 16g | Protein: 20g |
Fat: 13g | Fiber: 5g

SERVINGS: 8

INGREDIENTS

- 1 ½ Pounds 80/20 Hamburger
- 1 28 Ounce Can Diced Tomatoes
- 1 8 Ounce Can Tomato Sauce
- 1 15.5 Ounce Can Light Red Kidney Beans (optional)
- 1 10 Ounce Bag Frozen Seasoning Blend
- 1 Cup Frozen Riced Cauliflower
- 3 Tablespoons Chili Powder
- 1 Tablespoon Garlic Powder
- 2 Teaspoons Cumin
- ½ Teaspoon Oregano
- ½ Teaspoon Crushed Red Pepper (optional)
- 1 ½ Cups Water

INSTRUCTIONS

1. Add all ingredients to pressure cooker, adding beef last.
2. Close pressure cooker lid and seal.
3. Process at manual pressure for 35 minutes if using frozen beef, or 15 minutes if using thawed ground beef.
4. Quick Pressure Release.
5. Remove beef and crumble it (break it up), then return it to the chili.
6. Serve with optional toppings of sour cream, shredded cheese, and green onions.

Alfredo Sauce

Nutrition - 1/2 Cup
Calories: 288 | Carbohydrates: 3g | Protein: 5g |
Fat: 28g | Fiber: 0g

SERVINGS: 6

INGREDIENTS

- 2 Tablespoons Butter
- 5 Cloves Garlic, Crushed/Minced
- 1 ½ Cups Heavy Whipping Cream
- 1 Cup Chicken Bone Broth
- 1 Cup Grated Parmesan (I used the fine grated - in a green can)
- Salt, to taste

INSTRUCTIONS

1. In a medium skillet, melt butter and saute garlic for 1-2 minutes.
2. Add heavy cream and bone broth, stirring well.
3. Add Parmesan and stir again.
4. Reduce heat and simmer for 5-10 minutes, or until sauce begins to thicken.
5. Add salt, to taste.

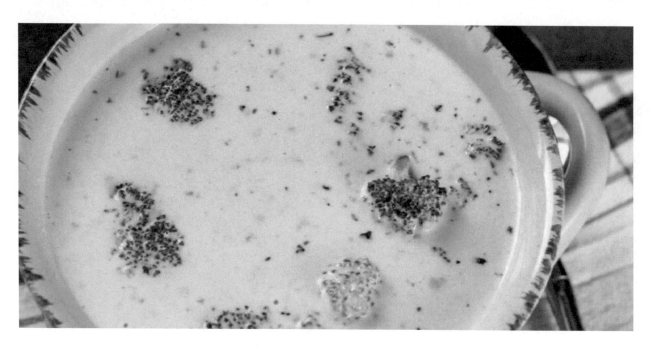

Broccoli Alfredo Soup with Sausage

Nutrition - 1/6th of recipe
Calories: 584 | Carbohydrates: 48g | Protein: 24g |
Fat: 38g | Fiber: 1g

SERVINGS: 4

INGREDIENTS

- 1 Pound Italian Sausage
- 1/2 Cup chopped onion
- 1 Tablespoon chopped jalapeno
- 2 Cups Chicken bone broth
- 1 Recipe low carb Alfredo sauce
- 2 Cups chopped fresh broccoli
- 2 Teaspoons Italian seasoning
- 1/8 Teaspoon Glucomannan

INSTRUCTIONS

1. In a large stockpot, brown sausage with onion and optional jalapeño.
2. Drain well, but do not rinse.
3. Add bone broth, Alfredo sauce, broccoli, and Italian seasoning, and bring to a slow simmer.
4. Heat just until the broccoli is tender and the soup is heated through. (Be careful that you heat slowly, so the cream does not separate.)
5. Whisk in Glucomannan and simmer for a few more moments, or until the soup begins to thicken.

Creamy Tomato Soup with Cream Cheese & Basil

Nutrition - 1/4th of recipe
Calories: 254 | Carbohydrates: 9g | Protein: 22g |
Fat: 7g | Fiber: 1g

SERVINGS: 4

INGREDIENTS

- ½ Tablespoon Butter
- ¼ Cup Onions, Diced
- 3 Cloves Garlic, Crushed
- 1 Cup Chicken Bone Broth
- 1 28 Ounce Can Petite Diced Tomatoes
- 1 8 Ounce Can Tomato Sauce
- 1 Teaspoon Dried Basil (or can use 2 Teaspoons Minced Fresh Basil)
- 8 Ounces Cream Cheese, Softened

INSTRUCTIONS

1. In a medium saucepan, over medium heat, saute onions and garlic in butter until softened - about two or three minutes.
2. Add chicken broth, diced tomatoes, tomato sauce, and basil.
3. Bring to a simmer.
4. Remove 3 cups of soup to a blender, and add softened cream cheese.
5. Blend until well combined, then return blended soup to pot.
6. If necessary, heat soup on stove until desired temperature is reached.

Buffalo Chicken Chili

Nutrition - 1/6th of recipe

Calories: 382 | Carbohydrates: 8g | Protein: 31g | Fat: 19g | Fiber: 2g

SERVINGS: 6

INGREDIENTS

- 2 stalks celery diced
- 1 small onion diced
- 4 cups Low sodium chicken broth
- 1 13.5 ounce can coconut milk
- 2 tbsp ranch seasoning mix
- 1/2 cup wing sauce
- 2 pounds boneless skinless chicken thighs, cut into bite size pieces
- 1 to 2 teaspoons xanthan gum for thickening

INSTRUCTIONS

1. Place all ingredients EXCEPT xanthan gum into the slow cooker. Stir to combine.
2. Cover the slow cooker and cook on high for 3 hours.
3. Stir in xanthan gum, if desired, and allow to cook an additional 15 minutes or until thickened.

Beef Stew (without Potatoes)

Nutrition - 1/8th of recipe
Calories: 202 | Carbohydrates: 9g | Protein: 23g |
Fat: 8g | Fiber: 3g

SERVINGS: 8

INGREDIENTS

- 4 Cups Leftover Cooked Beef Roast, coarsely chopped
- 2 Tablespoons Olive Oil
- 1 Pound Turnip Roots, peeled and cubed
- 1 Onion, diced
- 2 Carrots, peeled and diced
- 1 Cup Frozen Green Beans, optional
- 4 Cups Beef Broth
- ¼ Cup Tomato Paste
- 1 Teaspoon Dried Thyme Leaves
- 1 Teaspoon Xantham Gum

INSTRUCTIONS

1. In a large stock pot over medium-high heat, add the olive oil and vegetables.
2. Cook approximately 5 minutes, stirring often, until the vegetables begin to soften. Season with salt and pepper if desired.
3. To the stock pot, add the beef roast, frozen green beans (if using), beef broth, tomato paste, and thyme.
4. Bring to a boil over medium-high heat and cook for 10 to 15 minutes or until the turnips are fork-tender.
5. Taste for salt and pepper and adjust seasonings if needed.
6. Add the xantham gum to the beef stew and stir until it thickens.

Shrimp Alfredo

Nutrition - 1/4th of recipe
Calories: 594 | Carbohydrates: 6g | Protein: 12g | Fat: 52g |
Fiber: 1g

SERVINGS: 4

INGREDIENTS

- 3 Tablespoons Unsalted Butter
- 2 Cups Half & Half
- 1 Teaspoon Garlic Powder or minced garlic
- 1/2 Teaspoon Onion Powder
- 1/2 Teaspoon Mineral Salt
- 1 Cup Heavy Cream
- 1 Cup Grated Parmesan Cheese the kind in the green can
- 3/4 Teaspoon Glucomannan Powder
- 12 ounces Small Shrimp, cooked about 2 Cups

Notes

The Glucomannan will cause this to thicken more and more the longer it sits. Simply re-heat it to thin it out a bit.

The nutritional information is for 4 servings, without spaghetti squash.

To lower the calorie and fat count, you could use one cup of unsweetened almond milk in place of one of the cups of half and half.

INSTRUCTIONS

1. In a large skillet, melt butter over medium heat.
2. Add Half & Half, spices, and Heavy Cream.
3. Heat until almost simmering, then add Parmesan.
4. Heat until simmering, then slowly sprinkle Glucomannan Powder over the Alfredo mixture, whisking well to keep it from clumping.
5. Add shrimp and continue to simmer until the mixture thickens.
6. Serve over zucchini noodles or spaghetti squash.

Chicken Lo Mein

SERVINGS: 6 servings

Nutrition -1/6th of recipe

Calories 135 | Total Fat 3g | Total Carbohydrates 6g | Dietary Fiber 2g |Protein 18g

- 3 to 4 Boneless Skinless Chicken Breast, cut into thin strips
- 2 Tablespoons Olive Oil
- 4 Cups Broccoli Florets
- 1 Red Bell Pepper cut into thin strips
- 1/2 Cup Carrot Strips julienned
- 1 Medium Onion cut into thin strips
- 5 Medium Zucchini spiralized

For the sauce:
- 1 ½ Cups Low Sodium Chicken Broth
- 4 Garlic Cloves minced
- ¼ Cup Liquid Aminos
- 3 Tablespoons Oyster Sauce optional - you can also just use additional Liquid Aminos
- 1 Tablespoon PLUS 1 Teaspoon Rice Wine Vinegar
- 1 Teaspoon Ground Ginger
- ½ to 1 Teaspoon Xanthan Gum for thickening

1. Season the chicken with salt and pepper as desired.
2. In a large (12 inch or larger) skillet, wok, or dutch oven over medium-high heat, add 1 tablespoon of the olive oil and part of the chicken. Brown the chicken on both sides and cook through until done.
3. Repeat with the remaining chicken, adding oil if needed. Remove the chicken from the skillet but keep warm.
4. Add the remaining oil and the vegetables to the skillet.
5. Cook until the vegetables begin to soften, about 2 to 3 minutes.
6. Whisk together the sauce ingredients.
7. Pour over the vegetables and bring to a boil.
8. Add the chicken and toss together to coat in the sauce.

Notes
There is some added sugar in oyster sauce, so please be aware of that.

If you want to use a substitute, see below.
What can I use in place of oyster sauce and fish sauce?
There are many different options for substituting oyster sauce. I recommend using a soy sauce alternative, such as Coconut Aminos or a gluten-free tamari sauce.

You can even mix soy sauce and Worcestershire sauce together to give a little bit more flavor.

Green Chile Chicken

SERVINGS: 12 servings

Nutrition -1/12th of recipe

Calories 193 | Total Fat 14g | Total Carbohydrates 6g | Dietary Fiber 0g |Protein 14g

- 4 Boneless, Skinless Chicken Breasts , cubed
- 1 Teaspoon Chili Powder
- 1/2 Teaspoon Ground Cumin
- 1/2 Teaspoon Black Pepper
- 1/2 Teaspoon Salt
- 1/4 Teaspoon Garlic Powder
- 1 Can (28 ounce) Green Enchilada Sauce*
- 1 Can (7 ounce) Green Chiles , diced
- 1 Package (8 ounce) Cream Cheese , softened
- 2 Cups Shredded Monterey Jack Cheese , divided

Notes

Using a 28-ounce can of enchilada sauce leaves a lot of sauce in the final casserole, which is great for serving over cauliflower rice. If you desire a less soupy casserole, use a 14-ounce can.

1. Preheat the oven to 350 degrees. Prepare a (9x13) casserole dish with nonstick cooking spray.
2. In a gallon size freezer bag, shake together the dry seasonings. Add the chicken, sealing the bag. Toss the bag and knead the chicken until the spices are evenly distributed.
3. Dump the chicken into the casserole dish, creating an even layer with space between the chunks of chicken if possible.
4. In a large mixing bowl, beat the cream cheese until soft and creamy. Stir in half of green enchilada sauce, green chiles, and 1 cup of cheese. Spread over the chicken layer.
5. Pour remaining enchilada sauce over the cream cheese layer and top with remaining cheese.
6. Bake for 45 to 50 minutes or until the chicken is cooked through, the cheese has melted, and the edges are bubbling.
7. Garnish with freshly chopped cilantro, black olives, diced tomatoes, and diced avocado if desired.

Pizza Stuffed Chicken

Nutrition - 1/6th of recipe

Calories: 307 | Carbohydrates: 4g | Protein: 56g |
Fat: 10g | Fiber: 0g

SERVINGS: 6

INGREDIENTS

- 3 Large Boneless, Skinless Chicken Breasts (roughly 3 lbs. total)
- 30 Pepperoni Slices
- 1 Cup Shredded Mozzarella Cheese
- 1 Cup Sugar Free Pizza Sauce
- Salt and pepper, to taste

INSTRUCTIONS

1. Preheat oven to 375 degrees.
2. Spray a 9x13 inch baking dish with coconut oil cooking spray.
3. Slice chicken in half through the thickness of the breast horizontally and pound it to ½ inch thickness. (Avoid mess by placing chicken between sheets of plastic wrap or waxed paper when pounding.)
4. Sprinkle chicken with salt and pepper.
5. Add four slices of pepperoni and about 1 tablespoon shredded mozzarella to the middle of each flattened chicken breast piece.
6. Roll chicken, tucking the edges, and place in prepared baking dish.
7. Pour pizza sauce over each chicken breast. Top with remaining mozzarella and pepperoni slices.
8. Bake for 30 to 40 minutes (depending on the thickness of the chicken breast) or until a meat thermometer reads 165 degrees.

Cheesy Baked Chicken

Nutrition - 1/8th of recipe
Calories: 361 | Carbohydrates: 3g | Protein: 29g |
Fat: 25g | Fiber: 0g

SERVINGS: 8

INGREDIENTS

- 4 Boneless, Skinless Chicken Breasts
- ½ Teaspoon Salt
- ½ Teaspoon Pepper
- 1 Teaspoon Garlic Powder
- 1 Teaspoon Italian Seasoning
- 8 Slices Provolone Cheese
- ½ Cup Mayonnaise
- ½ Cup Sour Cream
- ¾ Cup Shredded or Grated parmesan cheese

INSTRUCTIONS

1. Preheat oven to 375 degrees. Spray a 9x13 baking dish with non-stick cooking spray. Place chicken in baking dish.
2. Mix together salt, pepper, garlic, and Italian seasoning. Sprinkle a small amount over chicken breasts. Top with sliced provolone cheese.
3. In a medium bowl, blend together the remaining seasonings with mayonnaise, sour cream, and parmesan. Spread over provolone.
4. Bake for 45 minutes to 1 hour, or until chicken reaches an internal temperature of 165 degrees.

Notes

Nutritional information and cook time will vary greatly, depending on the size of the chicken breast.

Please note that the nutritional information is for 1/2 of a chicken breast.

Lasagna Stuffed Chicken

SERVINGS: 4 servings

Nutrition -1/4th of recipe

Calories 454 | Total Fat 26g | Total Carbohydrates 9g | Dietary Fiber 2g |Protein 45g

- 4 Boneless Skinless Chicken Breasts butterflied (sliced partially through the width of the chicken breast, allowing one side to remain attached)
- 1 Tablespoon Olive Oil
- ¾ Cup Ricotta Cheese
- 1 ½ Cups Shredded Mozzarella Cheese divided
- ½ Cup Grated Parmesan Cheese divided
- 1 Large Egg
- Salt and Black Pepper to taste
- 1 Teaspoon Italian Seasoning divided
- 2 Cups Marinara Sauce

1. Preheat oven to 375 degrees. Prepare a 9x13 casserole dish with nonstick cooking spray.
2. Place ½ cup marinara sauce in an even layer on the bottom of the casserole dish.
3. In a small bowl, mix together the ricotta, 1 cup shredded mozzarella cheese, ¼ cup parmesan cheese, egg, and ½ teaspoon Italian seasoning. Mix until completely blended.
4. Mix the remaining Italian seasoning with salt and pepper.
5. Open the chicken breast and sprinkle lightly with half of the seasoning mixture.
6. Place about 1 tablespoon of the marinara sauce into the chicken.
7. Top with about ¼ cup of the ricotta mixture. Fold chicken over to close and place in the casserole dish.
8. Pour oil over the top of the chicken breast and sprinkle with remaining seasoning.
9. Bake, uncovered, in the oven for 30 to 35 minutes. Check the chicken for an internal temperature of 160 degrees. Remove from the oven and reset the oven temperature to Broil, preheating the broiler.
10. Using a baster, remove any excess juices or oil from the casserole dish.
11. Top the chicken with remaining marinara sauce, mozzarella cheese, and parmesan cheese.
12. Place the casserole dish under the broiler allowing the cheese to melt and the chicken to cook to an internal temperature of 165 degrees.
13. Remove from the oven and allow the chicken to rest for 5 to 10 minutes prior to serving.

Easy Chicken Cordon Bleu

Nutrition - 1/4th of recipe
Calories: 555 | Carbohydrates: 3g | Protein: 59g |
Fat: 35g | Fiber: 0g

SERVINGS: 4

INGREDIENTS

- 4 Boneless Skinless Chicken Breasts
- 8 Slices Black Forest Ham
- 8 Slices Swiss Cheese , cut in half
- 2 Tablespoons Dijon Mustard
- 2 Oz. Cream Cheese
- 1/3 C. Pork Rind Crumbs
- 2 Tablespoons Olive Oil
- Salt and Pepper to taste

INSTRUCTIONS

1. Turn oven to broil.
2. In a bowl, mix together the cream cheese and dijon mustard until smooth.
3. Place the chicken breasts into a casserole dish, and drizzle with the olive oil.
4. Season the chicken with salt and pepper to taste, and place under the broiler on high for 10 minutes.
5. Flip the chicken over, and broil another 10 minutes.
6. Remove the chicken, and top with 1 slice of the swiss cheese.
7. Add the ham to each piece of chicken, then top with the mustard sauce, before adding the remaining slices of cheese.
8. Place under the broiler for 2-3 minutes.
9. Sprinkle with the pork rind crumbs, and place under the broiler for another 2-3 minutes.
10. Make sure the chicken is cooked completely through before serving. Cooking time can vary depending on the thickness of your chicken breasts.

Pressure Cooker Garlic Parmesan Chicken

Nutrition - 1/6th of recipe

Calories: 339 | Carbohydrates: 2g | Protein: 31g |

Fat: 24g | Fiber: 0g

SERVINGS: 6

INGREDIENTS

- 3 Pounds Boneless Skinless Chicken Breast cubed
- ¼ Cup Olive Oil divided
- 2 ½ Teaspoons Italian Seasoning Blend
- ¼ to ½ Teaspoon Crushed Red Pepper Flakes optional
- 6 Cloves Garlic minced
- 1 Cup Chicken Broth
- ¼ Cup Freshly Grated Parmesan Cheese
- ¾ Cup Heavy Whipping Cream
- 8 Ounces Cream Cheese

Notes
You can skip the browning step but expect some of the meat to stick together in clumps. You will also need to cook for 8 minutes, instead of 3.

INSTRUCTIONS

1. Set the pressure cooker to saute and heat until "hot."
2. Mix together the dried seasonings and sprinkle over the chicken.
3. Into the hot pressure cooker liner, add olive oil and chicken in small batches to brown on both sides. Set aside and keep warm.
4. Pour chicken broth into the pressure cooker and scrape the bottom with a flat edged spatula or spoon.
5. Add the chicken and garlic to the pressure cooker.
6. Close and set the valve to sealing. Set the pressure cooker to manual or pressure cook for 3 minutes. Naturally release for 5 minutes before a quick release.
7. Stir in Parmesan cheese, cream, and cream cheese, allowing to cook until it thickens to your desired consistency.
8. Serve alone or over zoodles or spaghetti squash.

Pressure Cooker Taco Stuffed Peppers

SERVINGS: 4 servings

Nutrition -1 Stuffed Pepper

Calories 422 | Total Fat 25g | Total Carbohydrates 9g | Dietary Fiber 2g |Protein 41g

- 4 Medium Bell Peppers
- 1 Teaspoon Chili Powder
- ½ Teaspoon Ground Cumin
- ½ Teaspoon Smoked Paprika
- ½ Teaspoon Salt
- ½ Teaspoon Black Pepper
- 1 ½ Cup Water
- 1 ½ Pounds Ground Beef
- 1 Onion, Finely Diced
- 2 Cloves Garlic, Minced
- 1 Cup Shredded Fiesta Blend Cheese, Divided

1. Remove the tops, core, and seeds from each bell pepper.
2. Pour water into pressure cooker liner. Add the trivet over the water.
3. In the large bowl, add ground beef, seasonings, onion, garlic, and ½ cup cheese. Blend together well with hands. Divide into equal portions according to the number of bell peppers.
4. Stuff the meat mixture into each bell pepper. Position bell peppers on the trivet inside the electric pressure cooker.
5. Close the pressure cooker and set the value to sealing. Set the pressure cooker to manual or pressure cook on high for 8 minutes. When the cycle is complete, allow the electric pressure cooker to release naturally for 6 to 8 minutes before quick release.
6. Top each pepper with remaining cheese and cover until melted.
7. Carefully remove the bell peppers from the pressure cooker, allowing any excess liquid in the peppers to pour back into the pot. (Long handled tongs are especially useful.) Serve with chopped cilantro, limes, sour cream, salsa, avocado, or your favorite taco toppings.

Pork Chops with Mushroom Cream Sauce

SERVINGS: 4 servings

Nutrition -1/4th of recipe

Calories 556 | Total Fat 41g | Total Carbohydrates 4g | Dietary Fiber 1g | Protein 44g

FOR THE PORK CHOPS

- 4 Boneless Pork Chops (about 1.5 Pounds)
- 1 Tablespoon Refined Coconut Oil
- Garlic Salt, to taste

MUSHROOM CREAM SAUCE

- 2/3 Cup Heavy Cream
- 1 Tablespoon Butter
- 12 Ounces Mushrooms, Sliced
- 3 Garlic Cloves, Minced

1. Melt coconut oil in a skillet over medium heat. Add pork chops to pan and cook for three minutes.
2. Turn the pork chops and cook for three more minutes. (Or until the internal temperature is 145.)
3. Remove pork chops from the pan and place on a plate (cover with foil to retain heat).
4. Add the butter, mushrooms, and garlic to the pan and saute for 1-2 minutes.
5. Add the heavy cream to the pan and bring to a low simmer. Simmer for 3-5 minutes, or until sauce begins to thicken. (You can add a pinch of gluccie to help it thicken, if you desire.)
6. Return pork chops to the pan and simmer in the sauce for 1-2 more minutes.

Notes
If you would like to help the sauce thicken faster, you can add a pinch of glucomannan.

Cheesy Sausage & Cabbage Skillet

Nutrition - 1/4th of recipe
Calories: 356 | Carbohydrates: 5g | Protein: 19g |
Fat: 29g | Fiber: 2g

SERVINGS: 4

INGREDIENTS

- 2 Tablespoons Butter
- 1 Small Head Cabbage Sliced (about 8 cups)
- ¼ Cup Nutritional Yeast
- 4 Smoked Sausages
- Salt and Pepper to taste

INSTRUCTIONS

1. Preheat an iron skillet and melt butter. (You can use any skillet, but I love my iron skillet.)
2. Slice cabbage into thin strips and add to the hot butter.
3. Slice sausages and add to the skillet.
4. Sprinkle nutritional yeast over the sausage and cabbage.
5. Cook over medium heat for 5-7 minutes, or until cabbage begins to wilt and sausages are heated through.
6. Season with salt and pepper, to taste.

Notes
You can make this recipe dairy free by replacing the butter with coconut oil.
I like to sprinkle crushed red pepper over mine when I eat it!

Speedy Zucchini Bacon Alfredo

Nutrition - Entire Recipe
Calories: 271 | Carbohydrates: 7g | Protein: 12g |
Fat: 23g | Fiber: 1g

SERVINGS: 1

INGREDIENTS

- 1 Medium Zucchini Spiralized
- 1-2 Slices Bacon Cooked and Crumbled (or 1/4 Cup Pre-Cooked Bacon Crumbles)
- 1/4 Teaspoon Garlic Salt
- 1 Tablespoon Heavy Whipping Cream
- 3 Tablespoons Half & Half
- 3 Tablespoons Grated Parmesan Cheese (the kind from the green can)

INSTRUCTIONS

1. In a medium skillet, over medium heat, fry bacon until crisp.
2. Chop bacon into small pieces.
3. Drain bacon grease from pan, reserving a small amount if desired.
4. Make your "zoodles." (Spiralize the zucchini.)
5. Saute the zoodles and bacon pieces in the bacon grease for 3-4 minutes, or until the zoodles begin to soften.
6. Remove zoodles from pan.
7. In a separate saucepan, combine heavy whipping cream, half & half, and Parmesan cheese.
8. Heat until mixture begins to bubble and thicken.
9. Pour alfredo sauce over zoodles and serve.

Notes

If you do not want to use two pans, feel free to just add the sauce ingredients to the same skillet with the zoodles and bacon. Cook until sauce begins to bubble and thicken.

MY *Montana* KITCHEN

Bacon Wrapped Chicken with Jalapeno Cream Sauce

SERVINGS: 4 servings

Nutrition -1/4th of recipe

Calories 658 | Total Fat 51g | Total Carbohydrates 5g | Dietary Fiber 0g |Protein 49g

- 2 Chicken Breasts
- 8 Slices Bacon

For the Sauce:

- 4 Ounces Cream Cheese Softened
- ½ Cup Heavy Whipping Cream
- 1 Cup Unsweetened Almond Milk
- ½ Cup Grated Parmesan Cheese I use the green can variety
- 1 Teaspoon Onion Powder
- 2 Tablespoons Butter
- 1 Jalapeño Sliced (can use more if desired)
- 2 Teaspoons Minced Garlic

1. Preheat a skillet with medium heat.
2. Slice chicken breasts in half horizontally (so you should have 4 pieces of chicken).
3. Wrap two pieces of uncooked bacon around each piece of raw chicken.
4. Place bacon wrapped chicken in pan and pan fry over medium low heat for 20-25 minutes, turning several times to ensure even cooking and crispy bacon. Chicken should reach an internal temperature of 160.
5. Prepare Sauce:
6. In a medium bowl, mix softened cream cheese, heavy whipping cream, almond milk, parmesan cheese and onion powder.
7. When the chicken has finished cooking, remove from pan and drain bacon grease.
8. Add 2 Tablespoons butter to the pan and return to heat, scraping up pieces of bacon that are left in the pan.
9. Saute sliced Jalapeños and garlic in butter until Jalapeños are cooked through and garlic begins to lightly brown.
10. Pour prepared sauce into the pan and simmer for 10-15 minutes or until sauce has reduced a bit and begins to thicken.
11. To serve, top each piece of chicken with a generous amount of cream sauce.

Creamy Basil Chicken Thighs

Nutrition - 1/6th of recipe
Calories: 498 | Carbohydrates: 3g | Protein: 36g |
Fat: 38g | Fiber: 0g

SERVINGS: 6

INGREDIENTS

- 2 Pounds Boneless Skinless Chicken Thighs or chicken breasts
- 1 8 ounce Block of Cream Cheese softened
- 1 Tablespoon Butter
- 1/2 Cup Chicken Broth
- 1/2 Cup Heavy Whipping Cream
- 1/4 Cup Grated Parmesan Cheese from the green can
- 1/4 Teaspoon Mineral Salt
- 1/4 Cup Fresh Chopped Basil lightly packed
- Garlic Powder and Italian Seasoning to taste

INSTRUCTIONS

1. Season chicken on both sides with garlic powder and Italian seasoning.
2. In a skillet, brown chicken with a small amount of oil until cooked through.
3. Meanwhile, in a sauce-pot, melt softened cream cheese and butter. Whisk with a whisk until smooth.
4. Add chicken broth, whipping cream, Parmesan, and salt to cream cheese mixture.
5. Add chopped fresh basil to sauce and stir until combined.
6. Remove chicken from skillet, and drain drippings.
7. Return chicken to pan, and pour sauce over top.

Cajun Chicken Eggroll in a Bowl

Nutrition - 1/4th of recipe

Calories: 160 | Carbohydrates: 13g | Protein: 24g |

Fat: 2g | Fiber: 6g

SERVINGS: 4

INGREDIENTS

- 1 Pound Boneless Skinless Chicken Breast cut into pieces
- 10 Cups Chopped Cabbage 1 medium head
- 2 Tablespoons Yellow Mustard
- 2 Teaspoons Creole Seasoning
- 1 Teaspoon Smoked Paprika
- 1 Teaspoon Garlic Salt
- 1 1/2 Teaspoon Italian Seasoning
- 1 Teaspoon Chili Powder
- 1/2 Teaspoon Liquid Smoke
- 3/4 Cup Water
- Snipped Fresh Cilantro, optional

INSTRUCTIONS

1. In a large skillet, brown chicken.
2. When chicken is cooked through, add chopped cabbage, all seasonings, and water.
3. Stir, while allowing to cook for 5-10 minutes, or until cabbage is wilted to your desired tenderness.

Green Chile Chicken Enchiladas

SERVINGS: 10 servings

Nutrition - 1 Enchilada

Calories 329 | Total Fat 23g | Total Carbohydrates 24g | Dietary Fiber 26g | Protein 14g

Chicken Mixture

- 3 Cups Cooked Shredded Chicken
- 1 Cup Salsa Verde
- 1 1/2 Teaspoons Cumin Divided
- 1/2 Cup Chopped Cilantro Divided

Sauce

- 8 Ounces Cream Cheese, Softened
- 1/2 Cup Plain Greek Yogurt
- 1/2 Cup Cottage Cheese
- 1/2 Cup Unsweetened Almond Milk
- 1/2 Teaspoon Chili Powder
- 1 Teaspoon Garlic Salt
- 1 Jalapeno Seeded
- 7 Ounce Can Green Chiles

Other Ingredients

- 10 Low Carb Tortillas (I like Mission brand)
- 2 Cups Shredded Cheddar Cheese

1. Preheat oven to 350.
2. Mix shredded chicken with salsa verde, 1/2 teaspoon cumin, and 1/4 cup chopped fresh cilantro.
3. Fill each low-carb tortilla with the chicken mixture, and 1-2 Tablespoons of cheese.
4. Roll tortillas and place in a greased 9x13 dish.
5. Make Sauce
6. Place softened cream cheese, greek yogurt, cottage cheese, unsweetened almond milk, garlic salt, 1 teaspoon cumin, chili powder, seeded jalapeno, green chiles, and remaining 1/4 cup chopped cilantro in a blender. Blend until you have a creamy sauce.
7. Pour sauce over the enchiladas and top with remaining cheese.
8. Bake in preheated oven for 25-30 minutes, or until cheese begins to turn golden brown.
9. Serve with your favorite toppings.

Low-Carb Multi-Purpose Dough

Nutrition - 1/4th of recipe
Calories: 209 | Carbohydrates: 14g | Protein: 12g |
Fat: 10g | Fiber: 4g

SERVINGS: 4

INGREDIENTS

- 1 ½ Cups Plus 2/3 Cup Shredded Mozzarella Cheese, divided
- 2 Tablespoons Cream Cheese
- 1 egg

Notes
This recipe also makes a great pizza crust!

INSTRUCTIONS

1. Preheat the oven to 400F degrees.
2. Place 1 ½ cups shredded mozzarella cheese and 2 Tablespoons Cream Cheese into a large microwave safe bowl.
3. Microwave on high for 30 seconds. Stir well, then continue to microwave in 15 second increments, stirring between each increment, until the cheeses are completely melted. Stir until smooth.
4. Stir in the egg and almond flour.
5. Combine the dough in the bowl with clean, oiled hands until all ingredients are very well incorporated and it forms a ball. The dough will be very sticky. (You can also use a food processor for this step)

61

Chicken Bundles

Nutrition - 1 Bundle
Calories: 257 | Carbohydrates: 6g | Protein: 19g |
Fat: 18g | Fiber: 4g

SERVINGS: 6

INGREDIENTS

- 1 Recipe Low-Carb Multi-Purpose Dough (pg. 61)
- 1 Cup Shredded Chicken
- 4 Ounces Softened Cream Cheese
- 1 Tablespoon Plain Greek Yogurt
- 3/4 Teaspoon Dried Dill Weed
- 2 Tablespoons Chopped Onion
- 1 Stalk Celery Diced
- For Topping:
- 1 Egg Beaten
- 1 1/2 Teaspoon Grated Parmesan Cheese
- Extra Dried Dill Weed

Notes
If you do not have the Trim
Healthy Mama Baking Blend, you
can substitute all almond flour.

INSTRUCTIONS

1. Preheat oven to 400.
2. Mix chicken with cream cheese, yogurt, dill, onion, and celery.
3. Make Low-Carb Dough and divide the dough into 6 pieces.
4. On parchment paper, roll each piece into an approximately 6 inch circle.
5. Place approximately 2 Tablespoons of chicken mixture in the middle of each circle.
6. Pull up the edges of the dough and seal at the top (see video above for a photo).
7. Place on a parchment lined cookie dough sheet (I used my silicone mat).
8. Brush the tops of the bundles with beaten egg.
9. Sprinkle the tops of the bundles with the grated parmesan cheese and a sprinkle of extra dill.
10. Bake for 15 minutes, or until tops begin to turn golden brown.

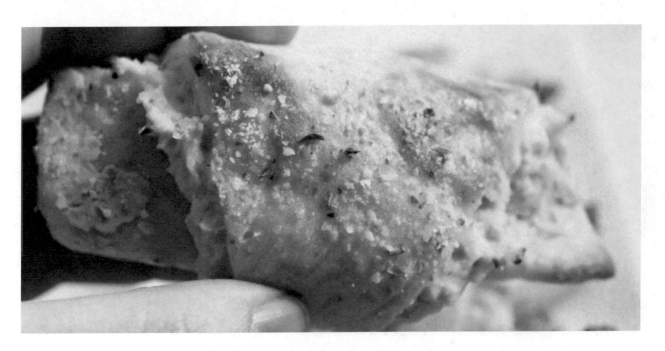

Buffalo Chicken Crescents

Nutrition - 1 Crescent
Calories: 232 | Carbohydrates: 5g | Protein: 15g |
Fat: 18g | Fiber: 1g

SERVINGS: 8

INGREDIENTS

- 1 Recipe Low Carb Multi-Purpose Dough (pg. 61)
- 1 1/2 Cups Cooked Shredded Chicken
- 1 Tablespoon Chopped Onion
- 4 Ounces Cream Cheese Softened
- 1/2 Cup Plain Greek Yogurt
- 3 Tablespoons of your favorite hot sauce I used Tabasco
- 1/2 Teaspoon Oregano
- 1/2 Teaspoon Garlic Salt
- 1 Egg White Whisked (for an egg wash)

INSTRUCTIONS

1. Preheat the oven to 400.
2. Make the Low Carb Dough.
3. Mix the chicken, onion, softened cream cheese, yogurt, hot sauce, oregano and garlic salt together.
4. Between two pieces of parchment paper, roll the Stromboli Dough into a large circle.
5. Using a sharp knife or a pizza cutter, cut the dough into eight triangles (as you would cut a pizza).
6. Divide the chicken mixture evenly and place on the dough triangles.
7. Beginning at the wide end, slowly roll the crescents up.
8. Brush the whisked egg white on top of the crescents, and top with additional seasonings, if desired.
9. Bake for 15-20 minutes, or until tops begin to turn golden brown.

Cheddar Jalapeno Meatloaf Muffins

Nutrition - 2 Meatloaf Muffins
Calories: 282 | Carbohydrates: 7g | Protein: 18g |
Fat: 21g | Fiber: 3g

SERVINGS: 6

INGREDIENTS

- 1 Pound 80/20 Ground Beef
- 2 Eggs
- 1 Tablespoon Liquid Smoke
- 1 Teaspoon Mineral Salt
- 1 Teaspoon Garlic Powder
- 1 Teaspoon Onion Powder
- ¼ Cup Chopped Jalapeños plus more for topping
- ¾ Cup Shredded Sharp Cheddar Cheese Divided

INSTRUCTIONS

1. Preheat oven to 350.
2. In a large bowl, combine burger, eggs, liquid, smoke, mineral salt, garlic powder, onion powder, 1/4 cup chopped jalapeños, and 1/2 cup shredded cheddar cheese. Mix until well combined.
3. Distribute meat mixture evenly among the wells of a greased 12 cup muffin tin.
4. Top with slices of jalapeño and the remaining shredded cheddar cheese.
5. Bake for 20 minutes.

Chili Cheese Fries

Nutrition - 1/4th of recipe
Calories: 288 | Carbohydrates: 13g | Protein: 13g |
Fat: 20g | Fiber: 6g (does not include toppings)

SERVINGS: 4

INGREDIENTS

For the Fries

- 1 Large Jicama
- 1 Cup Refined Coconut Oil
- Tony Chachere's Original Creole Seasoning

For the Chili

- 1/2 Pound Ground Beef
- 2 Tablespoons Diced Onion
- 1 Cup Diced Tomatoes
- 1/2 Cup Crushed Tomatoes
- 1/2 Tablespoon Chili Powder
- 1/2 Teaspoon Cumin Poweder
- 1/2 Teaspoon Oregano
- 1/2 Teaspoon Onion Powder
- 1 Teaspoon Garlic Powder
- 1/4 Teaspoon Mineral Salt

Toppings

- 1 Cup Shredded Cheese of Choice
- Sliced Jalapenos optional
- Sour Cream

INSTRUCTIONS

For Chili

1. Brown ground beef/venison with onion until no longer pink.
2. Add remaining ingredients and bring to a simmer.
3. Simmer for 5-10 minutes, adding a bit of water if it gets too dry.

For Fries

1. Heat 1 cup of coconut oil in an iron skillet (over medium heat).
2. Peel jicama and slice into matchsticks (fries). (You will want them fairly thin so they will cook faster.)
3. Place sliced jicama in ice water and let sit for at least 10 minutes.
4. Drain jicama.
5. Fry jicama in batches in hot oil, removing when they begin to turn light brown (this took about 10-15 minutes for me).
6. Place on paper towels to drain, and immediately sprinkle with Tony's Creole Seasoning.
7. When all fries are finished, divide onto four plates and add optional toppings.

Porcupine Meatballs

Nutrition - 5 Meatballs
Calories: 245 | Carbohydrates: 10g | Protein: 22g |
Fat: 12g | Fiber: 3g

SERVINGS: 6

INGREDIENTS

- 2.5 Pounds Ground Beef
- 1 (12 ounce) Bag Chopped Cauliflower Rice
- 1 Onion, finely diced, divided
- 1 Teaspoon Celery Salt
- 2 Tablespoons Dried Parsley
- 1 Teaspoon Garlic Powder, divided
- 1 Teaspoon Black Pepper
- 1 Egg
- 1 Tablespoon Olive Oil
- 1 (15 ounce) Can Tomato Sauce, divided
- 1 Cup Water or Beef Broth
- 2 Tablespoons Worcestershire Sauce

INSTRUCTIONS

1. In a large mixing bowl, combine beef, cauliflower, half of the onion, celery salt, ½ teaspoon garlic powder, dried parsley, black pepper, egg, and 2 tablespoons tomato sauce.
2. Shape into meatballs.
3. Set electric pressure cooker to "saute" function until hot.
4. Add olive oil, onion and remaining ½ teaspoon garlic powder.
5. Cook until softened, stirring often.
6. Pour beef broth or water into the pressure cooker and scrape the bottom to remove stuck bits.
7. Stir in tomato sauce and worcestershire sauce.
8. Add meatballs and cover with lid, setting the pressure valve to sealing. Set to cook on "pressure cook" or "manual" for 15 minutes at high pressure.
9. When the cycle completes, quick release or allow pressure to release naturally. Serve meatballs topped with sauce.

Low-Carb Biscuits

Nutrition - 1 Biscuit
Calories: 69 | Carbohydrates: 4g | Protein: 4g |
Fat: 5g | Fiber: 4g

SERVINGS: 12

INGREDIENTS

- 1 Cup Trim Healthy Mama Baking Blend
- 3 Tablespoons Cold Butter
- 2 Teaspoons Baking Powder
- ¼ Teaspoon Salt
- ½ Cup + 2 Tablespoons Unsweetened Almond Milk
- ½ Cup Shredded Mozzarella Cheese
- 1 Egg
- ¼ Cup Egg Whites

Notes
If you do not have the Trim Healthy Mama Baking Blend, you can use 1/3 cup each of coconut flour, almond flour, and flaxmeal.

INSTRUCTIONS

1. Preheat oven to 375.
2. In a large bowl, mix Baking Blend, baking powder, and salt.
3. Using a pastry cutter, cut in butter until you have a crumb-like mixture, and the butter pieces are about the size of peas.
4. Add remaining ingredients and stir just until incorporated.
5. Drop onto a parchment lined cookie sheet. (Or you can use a Silpat mat)
6. Bake for 10-12 minutes, or until tops begin to turn golden brown. (I like to broil mine for the last minute or two to crisp the tops.)

Sausage Gravy

Nutrition - 1/6th of recipe
Calories: 364 | Carbohydrates: 5g | Protein: 24g | Fat: 29g | Fiber: 4g

SERVINGS: 6

INGREDIENTS

- 1 ½ Pounds Breakfast Sausage
- ½ Cup Trim Healthy Mama Baking Blend
- 1 ½ Cups Unsweetened Almond Milk
- ½ Cup Heavy Whipping Cream
- ½ Teaspoon Salt
- ¼ Teaspoon Black Pepper

INSTRUCTIONS

1. In a large skillet, brown sausage over medium heat. (Do not drain.)
2. Sprinkle Baking Blend over cooked sausage, and stir to coat.
3. Add remaining ingredients and stir well.
4. Bring to a low boil, reduce heat and simmer until thickened. (About 10 minutes.)
5. Enjoy with Low Carb Biscuits!

Notes

The nutrition information for this recipe is calculated using a generic bulk pork sausage - nutrition facts may vary depending on what sausage you use.

If you do not have the Trim Healthy Mama Baking Blend, you can probably use 3 Tablespoons each of Almond Flour, Coconut Flour, and Flax Meal.

Pizza Brunch Casserole

Nutrition - 1/12th of recipe
Calories: 151 | Carbohydrates: 2g | Protein: 11g | Fat: 11g |
Fiber: 0g

SERVINGS: 12

INGREDIENTS

- 1/2 Cup Marinara Sauce
- 1/4 Teaspoon Italian Seasoning
- 1 5 Ounce Package Mini Pepperoni
- 2 Cups Mozzarella Cheese shredded
- 8 Eggs
- Salt and Pepper to taste

INSTRUCTIONS

1. Preheat the oven to 350 degrees. Prepare a 9x13 casserole dish with nonstick cooking spray.
2. In a large bowl, mix together the marinara and Italian seasoning. To this mixture, add the pepperoni and mozzarella cheese. Stir to evenly distribute the ingredients.
3. In a medium bowl, whisk eggs until well blended. Beat in salt and pepper.
4. Stir the eggs into the pepperoni mixture until evenly blended.
5. Transfer the mixture to the casserole dish and spread in an even layer.
6. Bake for 45 minutes or until the center is set.

Bacon & Eggs Cottage Casserole

Nutrition - 1/8th of recipe
Calories: 181 | Carbohydrates: 4g | Protein: 18g |
Fat: 10g | Fiber: 0g

SERVINGS: 8

INGREDIENTS

- 2 Cups Cottage Cheese
- 6 Eggs
- 1 Teaspoon Garlic Powder
- 1/2 Teaspoon Black Pepper
- 1/4 Teaspoon Thyme
- 1 Teaspoon Mineral Salt
- 1/4 Cup Diced Onion
- 1/2 Cup Real Bacon Pieces
- 1 Cup Frozen Spinach, thawed and drained
- 1 1/4 Cups Shredded Colby Jack Cheese

INSTRUCTIONS

1. Preheat oven to 350.
2. Combine first seven ingredients in a blender and blend well.
3. Add spinach, bacon, and 1 cup of cheese and pulse blend until incorporated.
4. Pour into a greased cast iron skillet or 8X8 glass pan.
5. Top with remaining 1/4 cup cheese.
6. Bake for approximately 40-50 minutes, or until middle is completely set.

Ham & Cheese Casserole

Nutrition - 1/8th of recipe
Calories: 328 | Carbohydrates: 3g | Protein: 21g |
Fat: 25g | Fiber: 0g

SERVINGS: 8

INGREDIENTS

- 2 Packages (8 Ounce) Diced Ham
- 1/2 Cup Mayonnaise
- 2 Tablespoons Prepared Mustard
- 2 Cups Shredded Cheddar Cheese
- 8 Eggs
- Salt And Pepper (To Taste)

INSTRUCTIONS

1. Preheat the oven to 350 degrees. Prepare a 9x13 casserole dish with nonstick cooking spray.
2. In a large bowl, mix together the ham, mayonnaise, mustard, and cheese. Stir to evenly distribute the ingredients.
3. In a medium bowl, whisk eggs until well blended. Beat in salt and pepper.
4. Stir the eggs into the ham mixture until evenly blended.
5. Transfer the mixture to the casserole dish and spread in an even layer.
6. Bake for 45 minutes or until the center is set.

Thank you for your purchase!
As a FREE BONUS, I'm giving you a download of my best-selling ebook, "Easy 30 Minute Recipes"

Just scan here to download!

Made in United States
Troutdale, OR
11/12/2024

24722761R00042